CHRISTMAS
around the world

CHRISTMAS around the world

by
Emily Kelley

pictures by
Priscilla Kiedrowski

Carolrhoda Books · Minneapolis, Minnesota

*To my family and the memory of my dad,
and especially to my Sam*   — E.K.

For George and my mother, *God Jule!*
                — P.K.

Manufactured in the United States of America

This book is available in two editions:
Library binding by Carolrhoda Books, Inc.
Soft cover by First Avenue Editions
241 First Avenue North
Minneapolis, Minnesota 55401

LIBRARY OF CONGRESS CATALOGING-IN-PUBLICATION DATA

Kelley, Emily.
  Christmas around the world.

  (A Carolrhoda on my own book)
  Summary: Describes Christmas traditions in Mexico,
Iran, China, Sweden, Iraq, Spain, and Norway.
  1. Christmas—Juvenile literature. [1. Christmas]
I. Kiedrowski, Priscilla, ill. II. Title. III. Series.
GT4985.5.K44 1986   394.2′68282   85-13260
ISBN 0-87614-249-8 (lib. bdg.)
ISBN 0-87614-453-9 (pbk.)

  2 3 4 5 6 7 8 9 10 94 93 92 91 90 89 88 87 86

Contents

Christmas is the celebration of the birth of Jesus Christ. Almost 2,000 years ago, a carpenter named Joseph and his wife, Mary, lived in Nazareth, a town in Palestine. Mary was about to have a child. Christians believe that an angel had come to Mary and told her she would give birth to the Son of God.

At that time, Palestine was ruled by the Romans. Their emperor had ordered that a list called a census be made of everyone in the Roman Empire. So Mary and Joseph had to go to Bethlehem to add their names to the census. When they arrived in the town, there was no room for them inside the inn. But one innkeeper allowed them to stay in the stable, where Mary gave birth to her son, Jesus. They made a bed for him in the animals' manger. Many shepherds came to see Jesus in the stable. They said angels in the sky had sung to them about this special baby. From far away, three wise men came to give him gifts.

Today, Christians around the world celebrate Christmas every December 25. In this book you will read about some of the world's most heartwarming Christmas customs. Some of these customs are ancient. Others are much newer. From country to country, people celebrate Christmas in many different ways. But one thing is certain. Christmas warmth and joy are the same for Christians everywhere.

In Mexico, Christmas is called
Navidad (nah-vee-DAHD).
The main celebration is
posadas (poe-SAH-dahs),
which means "inns."
For nine nights
friends gather together for a parade.
They carry small figures
of baby Jesus, Mary, and Joseph.
They carry lighted candles
and sing Christmas carols.

Each night one man
pretends to be Joseph.
He knocks on a house door.
The house stands for
a Bethlehem inn, or *posada*.
"Can Mary rest here?" he asks.
"No," he is told.
"The inn is full."
After first being turned away,
everyone is asked in for a party.
Posadas ends on Christmas Eve.
When Joseph knocks on the door,
he is told there is room
only in the stable.
Everyone comes inside right away.
They sing songs and say prayers.
The figure of baby Jesus
is put into a manger.

Then bells ring and whistles toot.

There is a big, happy party.

Afterward, everyone goes to church.

11

Each night of *posadas*,
children play the piñata
(peen-YAHT-uh) game.
A piñata is a jug.
It is often made in the shape
of an animal.
One piñata is filled with water.
Another is filled with confetti.
The best one is filled with toys,
candy, fruit, and gifts.
Now the piñatas are hung
above the children's heads.
One child is blindfolded,
given a stick,
and twirled around.
He swings with his stick.
Two misses, then—*Whack!*
He hits the piñata with water in it.
Everyone gets splashed.

Each child takes a turn
until the good piñata is broken.
Then everyone dives for the toys
and sweets.

Iran is where the three Wise Men
lived when Jesus was born.
It was called Persia back then.
When they heard of Jesus's birth,
they started out for Palestine.
They carried gifts for Jesus.
A bright star rose in the sky.
It led them to Bethlehem,
where they found Jesus in a manger.

14

Today Christians in Iran
call Christmas "Little Feast."
They begin a fast on December 1.
They eat no meat, eggs,
milk, or cheese.
It is a time for peace and prayer.
Little Feast begins
after church on December 25.
A favorite dish called *harasa*
(hah-RAH-sah) is eaten.
It is a chicken stew.
People in Iran do not give gifts
on Christmas Day.
But children always get new clothes.
They wear them proudly
at Christmastime.

In China, Christmas brings
a special glow.
The Christians light their houses
with beautiful paper lanterns.
Their Christmas trees are called
"trees of light."
They are decorated with paper chains,
paper flowers, and paper lanterns.

Santa Claus visits China too.
He is called Dun Che Lao Ren
(dwyn-chuh-lah-oh-run).
Children hang up muslin stockings.
They hope Dun Che Lao Ren will come
and fill them with presents.

In Sweden, Christmastime
begins on December 13.
This is St. Lucia Day.
St. Lucia was a brave young woman
who lived in the fourth century.
Many people then
didn't like Christians.
So the Christians
had to hide in dark tunnels.
St. Lucia carried food
to them every night.
She wore candles on her head
to light the way.

On St. Lucia Day, Swedes
celebrate the Festival of Light.
Long before sunrise,
the oldest girl in the family
dresses all in white.
She puts an evergreen wreath
with seven lighted candles
on her head.
She carries coffee and buns
to her family in their rooms.
On Christmas Eve,
the family has a special dinner.
They usually eat ham and fish.
Then everyone opens their gifts.
On Christmas Day,
they will go to church
and relax afterward.

In Iraq,
Christians celebrate Christmas
in a special way.
On Christmas Eve,
the family gathers together.
One of the children
reads about the birth of Jesus.
Others in the family
hold lighted candles.

After the reading,
a bonfire made of thorn bushes
is lit in the yard.
It means good luck for the coming year
if the thorns burn to ashes.
Everyone sings
while the fire burns.
When the fire dies,
everyone jumps over the ashes
three times.
Each person makes a wish.

On Christmas Day,
another bonfire is lit.
This one is in the churchyard.
Then the church service begins.
The bishop comes in.
He carries a figure of baby Jesus
on a red pillow.
After the service,

28

the bishop blesses one person
with a touch.
That person then touches
the person next to him or her.
Everyone touches
the next person in turn.
Finally everyone has felt
the "touch of peace" on Christmas Day.

29

In Spain, most people go
to church on Christmas morning.
They spend the rest of the day
with family and friends.
On Christmas night,
one country custom in Spain
goes like this.
Many people go to the village square.

Here they find the "urn of fate."
Everyone writes his or her name
on a slip of paper.
The papers are put into the urn.
Then someone draws the names out,
two at a time.
Each pair will be best friends
for the coming year.

One very old Spanish custom
is still celebrated in Cadiz, Spain.
It is called "swinging in the sun."
Swings are set up
in the center of town.
The children of Cadiz take turns
seeing who can swing the highest.
They try to lead the sun farther north
so that winter will change into spring.

Twelfth Night is very important
to many people in Spain.
Twelfth Night is on January 6,
12 nights after Christmas.
It was 12 nights after Jesus was born
that the Wise Men first visited him.
On this night, children put
barley in their shoes.
Then they put their shoes
in doorways and on balconies.

The barley is
for the Wise Men's camels.
In the morning,
the barley is gone.
The Wise Men have left candy and gifts
in its place.

Many Christmas customs in Norway
began long, long ago.
One favorite custom starts
at harvest time late in the fall.
The best wheat is saved.
At Christmastime
it is put on poles
made from tree branches.
These make nice perches
for the birds.

A large circle of snow
is cleared away beneath each pole.
Norwegians say the birds dance
in the circle between meals.
This works up their appetites.
Just before sunset on Christmas Eve,
the head of the household checks
on the wheat in the yard.
If many sparrows are eating,
it means a good year for growing crops.

On Christmas Eve,
the family has a big dinner.
After dinner, it is time
for opening presents.
Then all the brooms in the house
are hidden.
Long ago, Norwegians thought
that witches and naughty spirits
came out on Christmas Eve.

They didn't want the witches
riding their brooms.
The fire shovel and tongs
are also hidden so the naughty spirits
can't play with them.

Spruce logs are burned in the fireplace.
The hot sparks will keep
witches from
flying down the chimney
into the house.
Lights are left on all night
to keep evil spirits away.
One bright light is lit
in a window to welcome
any Christmas travelers.
On Christmas Day,
most families go to church.
They spend a quiet day together.
This is a time for remembering.
They remember the reason
for Christmas warmth and joy.
They remember the birth of Jesus
nearly 2,000 years ago.

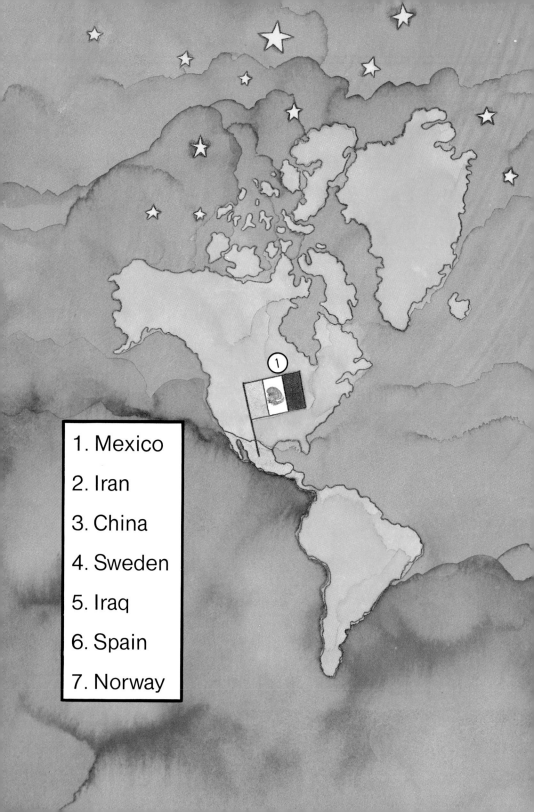

1. Mexico

2. Iran

3. China

4. Sweden

5. Iraq

6. Spain

7. Norway

Other Customs

Australia and New Zealand

Christmas comes in
summertime in these
countries. Families often
celebrate by having a
picnic at the beach!

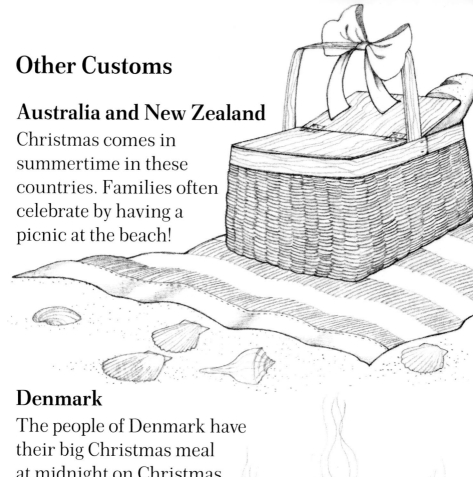

Denmark

The people of Denmark have
their big Christmas meal
at midnight on Christmas
Eve. For dessert they have
a special rice pudding
with one almond in it.
Whoever gets the almond
will have good luck in the
coming year.

France

On Christmas Eve, French children put their shoes in front of the fireplace. They hope that *Père Noël* (Father Christmas) will fill them with presents.

Germany

Besides lights, tinsel, and ornaments, German families put spicy cakes called *Lebkuchen* on their Christmas trees. These tasty ornaments are made in many different shapes.

CHRISTMAS JOKES

Q: Why are a lion at the beach and Christmas alike?
A: Because the lion has sandy claws.

Q. Why does Santa Claus go down the chimney on Christmas Eve?
A: Because it soots him so well.

Q. What does Santa Claus like to do in his garden?
A: He likes to hoe, hoe, hoe.

A CHRISTMAS CRAFT

Using colored construction paper,
trace and cut out three bells
exactly the same size.
Fold each bell the long way
down the center. Glue the sides
of the bells together to form
a three-sided ornament.
Hang it on the tree
or use it as a centerpiece.

GRANDMA JO'S CHRISTMAS COOKIES

1 cup powdered sugar
1 cup granulated sugar
1 cup butter or margarine
1 cup vegetable oil
2 eggs
1 teaspoon vanilla
4 cups plus 4 heaping teaspoons all-purpose flour
1 teaspoon salt
1 teaspoon baking soda
1 teaspoon cream of tartar

1. Cream sugars, butter, and oil until light and fluffy.
2. Add eggs and vanilla and mix well.
3. Sift together dry ingredients and gradually stir into butter mixture.
4. Cover dough and refrigerate for one hour.
5. Preheat oven to 350°
6. Roll small pieces of dough into balls and place on ungreased cookie sheet.
7. Flatten each ball with the bottom of a glass that has been dipped in red or green sugar.
8. Bake for 10 minutes or until golden brown.

Makes 5 dozen

Glossary

barley (BAR-lee): a kind of grain

bishop (BIH-shup): A high-ranking church official

carpenter (CAR-pen-tur): a person who builds things out of wood

census (SEN-suss): an official count of the number of people living in a certain area

confetti (kun-FET-tee): tiny bits of colored paper that are thrown during celebrations

emperor (EM-per-er): the head ruler of an empire

fast: to go for a period of time without eating certain foods

harvest (HAR-vest): fruits, grains, and vegetables that are gathered when they are ripe

lantern (LAN-turn): a kind of light that can be carried easily

muslin (MUZZ-lin): a kind of cotton cloth

urn (ERN): a large vase